MY WORLD, MY WORDS

Edited By Daisy Job

First published in Great Britain in 2022 by:

Young Writers
Remus House
Coltsfoot Drive
Peterborough
PE2 9BF
Telephone: 01733 890066
Website: www.youngwriters.co.uk

Book Design by Ashley Janson

Softback ISBN 978-1-80015-809-2

Printed and bound in the UK by BookPrintingUK
Website: www.bookprintinguk.com
YB0496G

FOREWORD

For Young Writers' latest competition This Is Me, we asked primary school pupils to look inside themselves, to think about what makes them unique, and then write a poem about it! They rose to the challenge magnificently and the result is this fantastic collection of poems in a variety of poetic styles.

Here at Young Writers our aim is to encourage creativity in children and to inspire a love of the written word, so it's great to get such an amazing response, with some absolutely fantastic poems. It's important for children to focus on and celebrate themselves and this competition allowed them to write freely and honestly, celebrating what makes them great, expressing their hopes and fears, or simply writing about their favourite things. This Is Me gave them the power of words. The result is a collection of inspirational and moving poems that also showcase their creativity and writing ability.

I'd like to congratulate all the young poets in this anthology, I hope this inspires them to continue with their creative writing.

CONTENTS

THE POEMS

Best Of Mankind

B est of humanity is he.
E very single one of us can see.
S o let's discuss a remarkable piece of art.
T he name 'Muhammad' - continually in my heart.

O f course, he was poor, yet he always loved to give.
F orever he taught the simplest way to live.

M ankind has learned so much from his regime.
A llah (SWA) has blessed him, made him so supreme.
N ot once did he commit a single crime.
K ept his word - morals of the sublime.
I f only I could see his face and shawl.
N ever would I have closed my eyes at all.
D eserves more praise, but the size of my poem is too small.

Adyan Rahman (10)
Al Mizan School, London

Myself

Me, myself and I.
The same and yet unique.
Me! Me! Me!
I am the centre of my parents' lives.
I am worth the effort.
I am the focus.

My efforts, my deeds, my sides.
I give my all.
I give too much.
I give more.
I give everything!

Myself.
Mindset is needed for balance.
Me, myself and I.
The same and yet different.
Myself.

Zaidan Rahman (7)
Al Mizan School, London

Animals

People have a pet.
Some are big and some are small.
Some even like to play with balls.
Once there was a cat I met,
So much black and white.
I asked my mum if I could keep him.
She said yes and I named my cat Dim.
I went out to fly my kite.
I met my friends at the park.
We played football on the hill.
Then, I went to the mill
And bumped into a loud bark.

Hamzah Miah (9)
Al Mizan School, London

Harry Potter

H umorous and happy
A fter all adventures.
R eady for dangers ahead.
R espectful to friends.
Y es, wins every match.

P lans are not ready but succeeds.
O utstanding all the time.
T ravel to save the day.
T rustworthy to everyone.
E xcellent for all things.
R egularly smart.

Mayisha Zauiahir (9)
Al Mizan School, London

Italy

It's a beautiful country and very humid,
The area is very ardent.
All of the food is super duper yummy.
Lots of people eat pizza as their snack.
You should visit all things.
As I love, I also hate mosquitos.
Not a good place when there are no tourists.
Do eat this food called Supplì.

Tahmid Razzak (8)
Al Mizan School, London

All About Benyamin

B enyamin is the name.
E xpert of London Underground.
N ervous and shy lots of times.
Y asmin Rashid's student.
A very behaved boy.
M oody quite often.
I like baking too.
N injago is my favourite TV show.

Benyamin Qasim (8)
Al Mizan School, London

Friends

F riends are everything.
R eally they are.
I love my friends.
E ndless friendship forever.
N ot enemies, friends.
D elicious food together.
S o we are besties.

Safiya Hannan (8)
Al Mizan School, London

How To Make Me!

Throw a heaped tablespoon of love,
Into a bowl of happiness and yeast.
Split into 6 parts,
And bake for 2 hours,
Add some icing and common sense.
Wait for it to rise,
And now you've made me!

Salmaan Al-Ameen (8)
Al Mizan School, London

Italy

I t's a nice place.
T oday, I would like to go there.
A nything is wonderful in Italy.
L ying in the sun is great.
Y ou can never be bored in Italy.

Afrin Sharmin (9)
Al Mizan School, London

This Is Me!

S afwan is me,
A nd I like talking a lot, it makes some
F uss.
W alking makes my leg ache
A nd I don't like to bake.
N ow I need to go.

Safwan Ahmed (8)
Al Mizan School, London

My Football Poem

I like football because I like balls.
First, you pass then shoot!
I want to be the best footballer in the world.
I come to school to learn and play.

Uzair Uddin (8)
Al Mizan School, London

This Is Me

Everybody says Khaleel is such a good boy and I am.
But I am so much more.
Being kind and caring to everyone is the main thing about me,
Helping others in need.
I am always gleaming with a happy smile and cheering others up.
My brain buzzes like a calculator,
Solving mathematical puzzles and tricky sums.
My responsibility is high and I am a capable big brother,
Watching over my little sibling, making sure they don't get hurt.
I am reliable and trustworthy when a friend asks me to do something.
I try to be honest but even though nerves get up my sleeves,
I am brave and courageous and always up for an adventure,
And hoping to peep at what excitement I see.
I am resilient and like having lots of fun in my mind and outside,

I like to ride roller coasters, zip lines and water slides.
Sometimes I can be emotional and sometimes sensible,
Even though I'm always dedicated and working very hard.
Also, my imagination is never behind bars.
Everybody says I'm a good boy and I am
But you can see
There is so much more to me.

Khaleel Ugharadar (9)

Bolton School Junior Boys, Bolton

I Come From Bolton

I come from a place where there are lonely streets.
I come from a place where my cats steal some delicious meats.
I come from a place where there are green fields and entertaining playgrounds.
I come from a place that owns friendly hounds.
I come from a place where people earn money by begging often.
I come from a place where there is always the rumble of cars.
I come from a place where rain pours down unexpectedly from the sky.
I come from a place where the wind roars when it passes by.
I come from a place where my neighbours have money that's golden.
I come from Bolton.

Ashton Morrissey (10)
Bolton School Junior Boys, Bolton

This Is Me

T his is a special poem about me.
H eroes that inspire me are named Rohit Sharma and Virat Kohli.
I like Lego and chess, which make me happy.
S ome of the other things I do,

I nclude cricket and football to name a few!
S cience, maths and history are my favourite subjects in the school day.

M y free time is when I get to chill and play.
E njoy being you and have a nice day!

Dhruv Patel (10)

Bolton School Junior Boys, Bolton

This Is Me

If I am to be so bold,
I will explain what it's like to be nine years old.
Homework and gaming are the order of the day,
Running long distance is my forte.
Wearing specs upon my face,
Books and maths I like to embrace.
Bolton School is like my second home,
The contents from which are a weighty tome.
I'm from Bolton School and I'm proud of it.

Joseph Stoddart (9)
Bolton School Junior Boys, Bolton

Hobbies

I am in a good mood,
When there is lots of food.
I like to run and play,
And game when it's a rainy day.
On the weekend, I walk and play in the park,
With my two dogs who bark and bark.
Football is cool and I'm on the team.
Could I play for Man City?
Well, that's the dream.

Theo Hodge (9)
Bolton School Junior Boys, Bolton

This Is Me

I am a football player.
I am a pizza eater.
I am a tiger lover.
I am as curious as a dog interested.
I am as smart as a meerkat.
I am as kind as a dog helping someone.
I am as chilled as a sloth sleeping in a tree.
My favourite colour is red.
My eyes are brown.
This is me.

Greenfield Jnr Chebelem Mufor (7)
Boston St Mary's RC Primary School, Boston

This Is Me

I am a great hugger.
I am a fantastic swimmer.
I am an animal lover.
I am an ice cream eater.
I am a tennis player.
My favourite colours are pink and
Colours in the rainbow.
I am a rainbow spotter.
I am a friend hugger.
This is me.

Grace Igwe-Omoke (7)
Boston St Mary's RC Primary School, Boston

This Is Me

I am a magnificent footballer.
I am a pet lover.
I am a pizza eater.
My favourite colour is orange.
I am friendly like a dog wagging its tail.
I am a rainbow spotter.
I am a sun hugger.
My eyes are blue.
This is me.

Jacob Sykes (7)
Boston St Mary's RC Primary School, Boston

This Is Me

I am a good swimmer.
I am a tennis player.
I am a cat lover.
I like pizza.
My favourite colour is green.
My eyes are brown.
I am a Pikachu painter.
I am a strawberry eater.
This is me.

Katrina Prasciunaite (7)
Boston St Mary's RC Primary School, Boston

This Is Me

I am a brilliant gymnast.
I am an apple eater.
I am kind, like a cat feeding its kitten.
I am a chicken nugget lover.
My eyes are blue.
This is me.

Viktoria Parasockaite (7)
Boston St Mary's RC Primary School, Boston

Tink The Dog

T ink is the best, but she is a mess.
H earts are together, besties love like a dove.
I love her so much.
S he is a licky dog, but I still love her like a glove.

I play with her all the time, like a mum.
S he likes to lick ice cream in her dream.

M y dog Tink, she's the best.
E yes glow in the dark, but she is a barky dog.

Kaselyn Pearson (7)
Christ Church Primary School, Newark

A View Of My Mind

I love aminals like a tiger.
I love Rainbow Dash.
I love watching TV with my mummy.
I like learning about Vikings.
I like going to Legoland.
I like cooking with my mum.
I love when the rainbow comes out.
I love dragons and wolves.
I love my pet Debelowe, he sleeps on his bed.
I like my friends and my teacher Mr Armstrong.
I like Halloween and the sweets.
I like strawberries with sugar.
I don't like falling over, haha.
I love autumn because leaves fall from trees.
I like playing duck, duck, goose.
I am really good at writing.
I am a big sister.
I am brave.
I am strong.
I am sweet.

I like reading books.
I like school.
I like after school club.
I like food.
I always play on the slide, *whee!*
I always fall over, haha!
I love watching Hatchimals, *eeh.*
I love winning.
I am a winner.
I love corn pizza.
I love running, *whoosh!*
I love being kind.
I love playing football with my friends.
I like playing Dragon Blast on the computer.
I like strawberry ice cream.
I eat watermelon and chocolate.
I have three sisters, two half-sisters and one whole.
I like playing on my scooter, *whoosh!*
I love going to school.
I love drinking hot chocolate and orange juice.
I love listening to Scooter.

I love old fashioned songs.
I like playing with Leo and Noah.
I love writing every day.

Sianna Mulley (7)
Christ Church Primary School, Newark

Oliwia Cooks

You will need:
A bag of animal love.
A sprinkle of sweets.
Cheesy pizza.
Some love and running milk.

Now you need to:
Add a bag of animal love.
A sprinkle of sweets.
Crunch the cheesy pizza.
Add love and running milk.
And stir it all up.
You can enjoy me with a movie or a picnic.

Oliwia Czekaj (8)
Christ Church Primary School, Newark

Things I Love

I love my hamster.
I love my mum and my dad.
I love vanilla ice cream with strawberry sauce with sprinkles.
I am a big sister.
I am good at cooking.
I am good at maths,
And I love to have baths.
I am great at flips on the trampoline.
I am good at singing.
I love pizza from Pizza Hut.

Shaniya Mulley (8)
Christ Church Primary School, Newark

This Is Me

I am a fast runner, *whoosh*.
I play FIFA and football.
My favourite football player is Ronaldo.
My dog is Teddy,
He is cute but he's messy and hiccups, it's funny.
My best friends are my little sister, she is soooo funny, and my baby brother, he is very very cute.
This is me.

Leo-Joshua Ring (8)
Christ Church Primary School, Newark

Chocolate Chomper

I am a cheeky chocolate chomper.
I love cheating like a cheater.
But I am a cookie cruncher.
Good game player.
Big bike rider.
Amazing apple cruncher.
I am a mess maker.
This is me.

Thomas Bolton (8)
Christ Church Primary School, Newark

This Is Me

I love playing with my dog.
I like cheese pizza.
I love my family.
I like my friends.
I like going to school.
I like to go on karts.
I like gaming.

Harrison Sutterby (7)
Christ Church Primary School, Newark

This Is Me

At playtime, I do the splits.
I know someone that knits.
My best friend is Sara.
She likes bananas.
My favourite colour is black.
It looks like a shack.

Evie-Rose Drewery (7)
Christ Church Primary School, Newark

This Is Me

I am very angry sometimes but,
When I eat melting chocolate,
I am happy.
I share my best moments with my mum and dad,
We like spending time together.

Kacper Poreba (8)
Christ Church Primary School, Newark

All About How I'm Unique

Hi, I'm Pareen and I am unique.
Now I am going to tell you all about me.
Now, first I've been dancing for 6 years,
And I really want to go forward into competitions.
Next, I want to become an author because,
I am good at Engish and imagine a lot.
A movie inspired me because there was a child that was writing spooky stories.
That was really cool.
Speaking about cool, my mum and dad are cool and the rest of the people I know.
My dad's a musician and he works with Indian singers and my mum has inspired me to become a young lady.
One of those Indian singers is Sonia Panesar,
And she gave me a poster.
That poster said:
I am strong
I am fearless
I am kind
I am unstoppable in English
I am brave

I am clever
I am resilient
I am equal
I am deserving.
I am loved, especially by all of my family,
Friends and teachers (Mrs Dev) (Mr Mcdonnel).
I am Pareen.

Pareen Singh (8)

Edison Primary School, Heston

This Is My Life!

I am the best of the best.
You know it's true.
Try beat me in a race or two.
I am kind and very nice.
I'll make you smile when you're feeling blue.
By the way that's my favourite colour too.
My name means the sun and I think you know why,
Because I am big and bright.
My hobby is handstands and I do them in my room.
But not just my room, but the school gates too.
My favourite teacher is Miss Dev,
She is the best and will help us on a test.
I like to dance to my favourite songs.
Favourite songs come on, come on, follow along.
I have a pet cat, he likes to eat rats.
I like plants, they make me feel happy and smart.
I am bright like the sun.
My name is Neferura

Neferura Sukaina Polley (8)
Edison Primary School, Heston

Gaming!

G aming is the best.
A t my friend's house, we play Minecraft.
M y mum doesn't let me play much.
I love to play Fortnite and FIFA.
N ever underestimate me in gaming.
G aming is the first thing I do when I'm bored.

I love playing Roblox too.
S adly, sometimes I lose.

T he best game in Roblox is Bedwars too.
H aving fun is my favourite part.
E specially having fun playing my favourite game.

B ecause I'm a sweat, I make a bet.
E specially in Roblox.
S adly, sometimes I lose.
T hat's my poem, I hope you like it.

Santi Sehgal (8)
Edison Primary School, Heston

This Is Me

It's me: Joshitha.
I wish to explore Antarctica.
I'm helpful and calm all day long.
My favourite colour is yellow.
Thieves are bad fellows.
I'd like to be a bear with very sharp claws.
The country I live in has some very strict laws.
My favourite songs are in hopscotch.
I like to eat butterscotch.
I like to play tag, my toy dog is called Wag.
I like to play football and I study in Goodall.
I like Dumbledore and I also like to dance on the floor.
I like to sleep and my favourite thing is to leap.
This is me and always fill your face with glee.

Joshitha Sunderavelu
Edison Primary School, Heston

My Halloween

I'm an eight-year-old boy,
Decorating my house with Halloween decorations.
When it is Halloween, I'm called the King of Halloween!
Devils, spiders, zombies and ghosts make me happy!
When people go into my house they go boo,
But when I turn on the ghost sound, they go *ooh!*
It feels like a graveyard in my house!
I give them spooky treats before they go.
But then I need to go for a dooky.
After that, I have the leftover pieces of candy.
Then my friend Mandy comes to my house,
And we have a lot of fun!

Joshua Prempeh (8)
Edison Primary School, Heston

This Is Me

My name is Sophia and I love having fun,
My skin is so shiny, it's as bright as the sun.
I have two dogs that are really cheeky,
They creep up on me so they're really sneaky.

I'm mixed race,
With beauty spots all over my face.
Some are hidden, some are not,
And I can't even tie my shoelaces in a knot.

I love playing games,
And my sister calls me names.
I have a gem collection,
And it has its own section.
Hello you leader, goodbye young reader.

Sophia Odjidja (8)
Edison Primary School, Heston

My Life

T his is me.
H e likes to watch TV, he is my brother.
I like gaming.
S paghetti is my favourite thing to eat.

I like dancing a lot.
S inging is one of my favourite things to do.

M y favourite colour is black.
Y ou might think it's strange but I like it.

L eopards are really cool.
I am about to finish.
F riends and family are the best things ever.
E agles are really fascinating.

Annabel Arjan (9)
Edison Primary School, Heston

The Monster

I'm a monster,
Taking down every poster.
I'm fearless
But very adventurous.

So don't doubt me,
Because most of the time, I'm angry
And messy.

I'm very, very lonely
But not silly
And very sad,
As well as bad.

I'm not very fun
Because my age is one hundred and one.
I'm not very kind
But I have a good mind.

I'm the monster
And this is me
And my poem.
I'm never happy.

Anxhelo Alia (8)
Edison Primary School, Heston

All About Me

I am wonderfully and fearfully made.
I am unique and special.
I like dancing a lot.
I am always comfortable talking with friends.
My favourite song is Faded by Alan Walker and the beat of Faded.
My second favourite is Dynamite.
I am crazy about books and reading.
I am also crazy about drawing and art.
I like learning new things and new stuff.
I like playing with my dogs, Shara and Sandy.
I like Mr Macdonal and Mrs Dev.
Now this poem has come to an end.

Josiah Pereira (8)
Edison Primary School, Heston

This Is All About Me

I am kind to my friends, teachers and family.
I am happy in the park.
I am brave in the night.
I don't get scared in the dark.
I am nice to everyone.
But I am sometimes silly when I dance.
I am having fun in the funfair.
My favourite things are dancing, drawing, playing and singing.
My favourite teacher is Mrs Dev.
I want to be a teacher in the future,
All thanks to my teacher.
My favourite colour is blue.
This is all about me!

Bahar Samsa (8)
Edison Primary School, Heston

All About Me

Hi, I am Hibba and I like to sing.
I also like the drums cause it goes *bing bang bing.*
I like the colour Mr Yellow.
Since he is a little tiny fellow.
I have dark brown hair which I take a lot of care.
I also like Mrs Brush because she tells me just to hush.
I like to paint, draw and play all day.
I also want to go fishing at the bay.
Well, thank you if you liked this rhyme.
But I think we have to say goodbye.

Hibba Wahid (9)
Edison Primary School, Heston

All About Me

I am the god of creativity.
I am good at any activity.
My favourite subject, art.
I love making tarts!

I love the colour blue.
It has so many hues.
Always speak the truth
Because your body gives clues!

I am kind,
But not out of my mind.
I am good at hide-and-seek.
Do not peek!

I love toast,
And I get the post.
I am curious,
But not furious!

This is me!

Akompreet Bansal (9)
Edison Primary School, Heston

The Sad Fat Fish

He was so sad and fat and got bullied.
He was shy at home with his mum.
He moved school and all the kids liked him.
He's so cool and he's not fat.
Magic happened and he turned into a human.
But then the bully came to his school.
He wanted to cry and others to make him happy.
But he stayed strong and kind.
So he was loved by everyone.
And he wasn't scared anymore.

Cyrus Kalsi
Edison Primary School, Heston

This Is Me

This is me,
Me is me.
Nobody can ever be me.

There is kindness and peace in our life.
We just need to find it by taking a breath and the love inside.

My name means fire.
Fire is scorching hot.
Sometimes I even think of it as a dot.

So my name is Diya,
Although my dad calls me Diya Piya.

This is me.
Me is me
And I love to be me.

Diya Mistry (8)
Edison Primary School, Heston

When I'm Sad

When I'm down I always play on my Nintendo,
It always takes away my frown.

When my sister does something bad,
It always makes me sad.
Sometimes she calls me a bum,
So I have to tell my mum.

Today I wore hair gel,
But it didn't really stay well.
Once, my sister got mad at me,
So she bit me then hit me.

Dhillon Arjan (9)

Edison Primary School, Heston

Imposter

I am Krrish.
M ondays are the worst because my sister calls me Trish.
P otions are my favourite because they give you powers.
O ceans are my favourite because I get to swim all day.
S hay is my best friend.
T ests are my worst fear.
E ating pears is a test.
R unning is the best.

Krrish Sharma (8)
Edison Primary School, Heston

Devan

My name is Devan.
I live in heaven.
I'm three years younger than eleven.

That means I'm eight, mate!
I'm a dude from the outside.
But rude from the inside.

D is for dancing.
E is for enthusiastic.
V is for valuable.
A is for amazing.
N is for nice.

Devan Tannk (8)
Edison Primary School, Heston

My Tortoise Is Called Angel

When I put water over my tortoise, she is sparkly.
She is green like a leaf with a bit of yellow.
She is a big grump but she isn't a dump.
When she falls down, she makes a big thump.
One time she nearly fell and cracked her shell.
She tried to escape but she realised that she got stuck.
Her shell looks like a belly.

Hannah Keay (8)
Edison Primary School, Heston

How To Make Me

Lots of happiness.
A sprinkle of smartness.
Another sprinkle of friendliness.
A pinch of sadness.
Finally some worries.
Almost forgot sportiness.

Mix the happiness with smartness.
A sprinkle of friendliness.
A pinch of sadness,
Mix some worries and add some sporty.
And you're done!

Bani Kaur (8)
Edison Primary School, Heston

This Is Me

I am kind like a flower.
I am strong like a lion.
I am brave like a warrior.
I love playing with my friends.
I have a dream, my dream is to make the world a better place.
I love ice cream.
I am nice to everyone.
I am afraid of dolls, they are scary like a ghost.
This is me.
I am Samaira.

Samaira Goes (8)
Edison Primary School, Heston

This Is My Life

I like reading books.
I like my teachers.
My favourite colour is light blue.
I don't like white.
My favourite book is Wizards of Once.
My favourite television show is Beyblade.
My little brother is four.
His birthday is two days before.
This is me.

Ammaar Anjum (8)
Edison Primary School, Heston

This Is Me

I am so kind to others.
I like learning.
I listen to whoever is speaking.
I listen to our rules.
I like to be polite to others.
I like to make others laugh.
I don't make fun of others.
I include everyone in my game.
Thank you for reading.

Muhammad Saadiq (9)
Edison Primary School, Heston

This Is Me, Shay

This is me, Shay.
I hate hay!

I love art.
It's my favourite part!

I love blue.
My brother found a clue!

I love food.
So when I am hungry, I get in a mood.

This is me, Shay!
And I hate hay!

Shay Gadher (8)
Edison Primary School, Heston

My Name Is...

My name is Micah and I like dancing.
My name is Micah and I like running.
My name is Micah and I like the dark.
My name is Micah and I like going to the park.
My name is Micah and I wish to fly.
My name is Micah and I like pie.

Micah Tamakloe (8)
Edison Primary School, Heston

My Favourite Colour

P ancakes are yummy.
I ce cream makes me happy.
N oodles are slurpy.
K itKat is tasty.

Simreen Kaur Budhraja (8)
Edison Primary School, Heston

Francesca

F rancesca is a kind, happy girl.
R oblox is my favourite game.
A rt is my thing.
N o, I want to go swimming, not the park.
C ooking is fun!
E xcellent at swimming.
S mart and sleepy.
C ats are better than dogs.
A wesome me!

Francesca Skinner (9)
Gesher School, Pinner

I Like Dogs

B rown hair.
E yes like a camel.
N ot a bat.

A lways full of energy.
N ever tired out.
D ogs do poos.

T ails wagging only when,
I t is quiet.
L icking.
L oudly.
Y uck, that is wet!

Ben (10)

Gesher School, Pinner

All About Leon

L ovely Leon likes Arsenal.
E xcellent Leon,
O nly Leon comes to school early.
N ever naughty!

Leon Krett (7)
Gesher School, Pinner

This Is Me

T he only daughter in my household.
H ave many annoying brothers that steal my food.
I have four dogs and cats and fish, so I have lots of company for me.
S o many sums to solve as I'm writing this poem.

I am an English hater and my brothers I hate too.
S ometimes I make brownies by myself, sometimes with my stepbrother.

M y favourite books are Harry Potter books, the Worst Witch and books by David Walliams.
E nergetically, I jump on my bed, ready to play Minecraft.

Lily Ricketts (9)
Littledean CE Primary School, Littledean

This Is Me

T ea, coffee, hot chocolate are my favourite hot drinks.
H appy is my usual mood, especially when I go on holiday.
I t is friends and family that mean the most to me.
S hopping all the time but spend too much money.

I love pizza, pasta, cucumber, cheese and fruit.
S chool, I love but sad to leave next year.

M ax and Harvey are my favourite singers.
E very night I dream of roller coasters and love Alton Towers.

Erin Rose Dunton (10)
Littledean CE Primary School, Littledean

This Is Me

These are things that describe me.
I like to read, it is so much fun.
Most of the things I dislike is poetry.
Hobbies and habits I have are staying up late and swimming as fast as a fish.
Friends and family are my world.
I've been called sporty, funny and strong.
I love learning and reading, especially Secret Seven and Harry Potter.
The people I would call my friends are Lily, Jonah, Kobe, Le-Bron and many more.
That completes the things about me.

Tianna Thompson (9)
Littledean CE Primary School, Littledean

This Is Me

T he most common thing people think about me
is chatty.
H appy like a dolphin, I can make you giggly.
I mmature with my funky jokes.
S mall in size, I can give you a few pokes.

I n my opinion, history and RE are the worst.
S ome of my favourite things are chatting and
drawing first.

M y favourite food is Super Noodles.
E ntertaining things are talking to friends and
poodles.

Caleb Light (9)
Littledean CE Primary School, Littledean

This Is Me

Hi, my name is Paighton, nice to meet you!
I really like art, don't know about you.
My favourite foods are ice cream and cupcakes.
Don't mind if I do!
Don't leave food hanging,
You'll find out why soon!
I have lots of friends, too many to list!
I dislike my brother Perry, very annoying indeed.
Thanks for reading my poem.
I'm going to have to leave.

Paighton Griffin (9)
Littledean CE Primary School, Littledean

This Is Me!

I want to tour the world,
To oceans deep and blue.
I'll find many a rare thing,
Like shining starfish and pearls so pure.
I'm going to the Amazon,
With its choir of birds,
And the Arctic where everything's exciting and new.
There are so many different things to try and test out.
But one of the real treasures about travelling,
Is coming home to you.

Chloe Swanson (10)

Littledean CE Primary School, Littledean

This Is Me

I don't like pickles, onions yuck.
In all the games I play, my friends have so much luck.
I like all my friends as much as TikTok trends.
I'm mostly outside whenever I'm not in school.
My dreams are of being tall.
Hobbies are English,
Whenever I'm not doing English,
I'm doing the dishes.
That was my poem.
I wish you liked it.

Tyler Crowell (11)
Littledean CE Primary School, Littledean

This Is Me

This is me,
My favourite colours are black, white, grey and red.
My favourite subjects are history, maths and PE in my opinion,
English is the worst.
I am ten next year on March the 1st.
My favourite food is pizza,
My least favourite food is Super Noodles, mushrooms and my mum's lasagne.
I would like to try pineapple on pizza.
Bye!

Lelan Meek (9)
Littledean CE Primary School, Littledean

This Is Me

T his is me,
H elping they say.
I am sporty, chatty but not brave.
S leeping I like because it's quiet.

I 'm terrified of gaming, it's dangerous.
S uper speed is my speciality.

M aths is fun-ish, it's okay.
E lephants go stomp stomp stomp, like my friend Tyler.

Reuben Averis (10)
Littledean CE Primary School, Littledean

This Is Me

I love art because art is my thing,
And if I don't have art,
Gaming's where I'll be.
Sport is one I am blessed to succumb,
Cricket and rugby consume me in love.
Happy and sad, gloomy and glad,
These are words to describe me.
So now I've wrapped up all the things that I am,
I must go enjoy all the things that I have.

George Nice (10)
Littledean CE Primary School, Littledean

This Is Me

T alking to my friends.
H elpful to my mum.
I nspiring.
S o this is so much fun.

I nteractive to new people.
S leeping is so good.

M y best friends are Olivia and Chloe.
E nding this poem, I'm going to be going.

Polly Bowkett (10)
Littledean CE Primary School, Littledean

This Is Me

T rix is my dog.
H appy as me playing Sonic.
I don't like walking.
S wimming like a frog.

I am funny and friendly.
S chool is boring.

M y favourite food is pizza.
E nglish is the one subject that is bad.

Jonah Crossfield (9)
Littledean CE Primary School, Littledean

This Is Me

T alking is my thing.
H ave a cute dog.
I love my family.
S till love Finland.

I love reading.
S easide, favourite place to be.

M ake cupcakes with my family.
E very Friday I have pizza.

Grace Partridge (10)
Littledean CE Primary School, Littledean

This Is Me

T all in size.
H ave been told I'm annoying.
I like sleeping.
S kinny like a twig.

I love Harry Potter.
S ometimes I hallucinate.

M aths is gross.
E ating is my talent.

Kala Mahon (10)
Littledean CE Primary School, Littledean

This Is Me

T winkle the tooth fairy book.
H elpful as a monkey.
I like going on my laptop.
S haring.

I love pugs.
S miling to help my friends feel better.

M aking food.
E ating.

Freya Whitmore (9)
Littledean CE Primary School, Littledean

This Is Me

T rolls.
H ave lots of pets.
I am good at Among Us.
S hort.

I am happy.
S cratch.

M inecraft.
E nderdragon.

George Watson (10)
Littledean CE Primary School, Littledean

This Is Me

I will forever be me, no one can stop me.
When I smile I light up the sky.
I'm generous, I'm kind.
I have dark green eyes.
I have bright ginger hair.
I'm as strong as a bull.
I can fly high.
When someone drags me down,
I stand back up and that tells me,
I'm a strong independent woman,
That is ready to take on the world.

Riley Millea (10)
Northern Saints Primary School, Sunderland

It's Me, Isla!

I want to be a professional dancer when I'm older.
S ome people think I'm a psychopath, they're not wrong though.
L ots of people think I'm mostly mature, but I'm actually very immature.
A nyone could think I'm just a normal human being, not in love with dogs but I love dogs!

T all people think I'm very short and yes they're correct.
O bviously poggers.
S o many people think I'm normal! I'm nowhere near 'normal'!
H airy spiders are disliked by me.
A n unnatural thing about me is I have annoying habits.
C akes make me feel sick.
K FC is very yummy, I love KFC!

Isla Toshack (10)
Oakdale Primary School, Stanground

This Is Me

My name is Ella,
I love mozzarella,
I'm a Harry Potter fan,
But not very glam,
Red is the best,
It's really my jest,
I'm as unique as a unicorn,
Slow as a sloth,
The best things are almost certainly soft,
I have seven pets,
No kidding, no sweat,
For me, friends and cheese,
Always fill me with glee,
I love to read books,
I could do it all day,
Ones about secrets,
Just don't give them away!
Now that is who I'm supposed to be.
Aha, that's positively, definitely me!

Ella Harradine (10)
Oakdale Primary School, Stanground

Finding Yourself

Enjoyment lies in the deepest places,
Big rooms and tiny spaces.
When I close my eyes in bed,
I don't know what will happen in the day ahead.
I'm crazy, cheeky and chatty too.
I'm not sure what I'll think of you.
Things can go left or right or even led astray.
In my world, things can go either way.
My brain is big, my legs are long.
I can either be weak or strong.
Pink is a part of me as much as my anatomy.
There's not much more I can say,
Apart from, I love to dance every day.

Daisy Madelaine Cockerill (11)
Oakdale Primary School, Stanground

This Is Lyla

I want to be a vet because
I like my animals.
I like cute and fluffy ones
Because they're the best.

I like to run all day.
Also I play, play, play.

I love pastel colours.
I want to be like no one else.
I express myself through history.
Like this will be sometimes I think a lot faster.

My favourite thing to do is to have fun.
I'm happy that I have courage,
So I can do something like this,
Life is true so succeed, succeed.
This is me.

Lyla Patten (7)
Oakdale Primary School, Stanground

This Is Me

I'm a boy.
I like reading books.
My favourite superheroes are Sonic and Spider-Man,
And Miles also Iron Man.
I like playing Roblox and Minecraft.
My favourite colour is blue.
I'm an awesome uncle.
My niece pulls my brother's hair while he's asleep.
I'm an amazing defender in my football team.
I play for Stanground sports.
My favourite food is garlic pizza.

Callum Wright (7)
Oakdale Primary School, Stanground

This Is Me

I am a superstar goalkeeper.
I can jump as high as the moon.
I am as fast as the Flash in football boots.
I am a brilliant skateboarder like Tony Hawk.
I love pandas because they are cute.
I have sky blue eyes like tropical water.
I like pizza, especially cheese.
I like nature because it makes me happy.
I am a football watcher,
Man United are the best.
This is me.

Jack Wright (7)
Oakdale Primary School, Stanground

My Favourite Animal

They live on the land but not in the sea.
They're not house pets, they run wild and free.
They're huge and black, much bigger than me!
They have colossal, sharp teeth.
Don't go near them when they're ready to eat.
They have no patterns, just plain colour.
If you go up to them, they will give you a runner!
What are they?

Answer: A panther.

Millie Lowder (10)
Oakdale Primary School, Stanground

All About Me

T iny in size.
H ave a habit of annoying people.
I 'm a super striker.
S ummer wishes here I come.

I love lots of sports, so you can count me as a sporty person.
S ometimes I'm quiet, only kidding.

M e and my friends playing.
E veryone likes me, I think so anyway. This is me.

Max Makuyana (10)
Oakdale Primary School, Stanground

This Is Me

I like football.
I'm a mid in football.
I like cricket.
I'm as quick as lightning.
My dog is a Jack Russell.
My dog is called Olly.
I'm a joke teller.
I'm a chatterbox.
I'm a super captain.
I like videos and video games.
I like the amazing Jurrasic Park.
I have a fish.
This is me.

Thomas Graham (7)
Oakdale Primary School, Stanground

The Giraffe

The giraffe, the giraffe with a long neck and lives
like Noah Beck.
He wrecks like a cannonball, breaks everything
with his long neck.
Short legs and likes to eat eggs every day, but not
all night.
He has a right to have his bright light.
Goes crazy but he gets really lazy.
My favourite thing, he always will stay just with
me.

Nicoll Miazga (10)
Oakdale Primary School, Stanground

About Me

I am... a good baker.
A better faker.
I have the best friends.
Our friendship never ends.
I'm a good gamer.
Never a blamer.
I love cats
And have good hats.
Not a good gun aimer.
An item claimer.
A dog tamer.
A music maker.
I once crossed the state.
I always finish a plate.

Matt Tamayo (10)
Oakdale Primary School, Stanground

This Is Me

T his is me and my life.
H itting and bullying are not okay.
I 'm kind and caring.
S inging I like.

I 'm loud and noisy.
S o like when I am dancing.

M y name is Anna.
E veryone in my family makes me happy

This is me.

Anna Harrison (7)
Oakdale Primary School, Stanground

This Is Me

Happy is what I am,
When I see my family.
Sweets are yummy,
Especially Fruit Pastels.
Minecraft is awesome.
I like finding diamonds.
Every time I see my nanny,
It makes me happy.

This is me.
I have brown hair.
I am kind.
I am happy.
I am quiet.
I am friendly.

Hugo Hunnybun (8)
Oakdale Primary School, Stanground

This Is Me

H appy.
A mazing smiler.
R eckless jokes.
R espect for all.
Y oung but powerful.

D awson is my surname.
A lways energetic.
W ill help others.
S uper striker.
O ver crazy.
N ever alone.

This is me!

Harry Dawson (10)
Oakdale Primary School, Stanground

This Is Me

I like turtles, they are so cute.
I love memories and places.
I like bees because they produce honey.
I love making art.
I like to sing.
I love rainbows.
I like pizza.
I love chicken.
I like rice.
I love coconuts.
I like books.
I love gymnastics.
This is me.

Amica Khan (7)
Oakdale Primary School, Stanground

This Is Important Me

I like pizza.
I have brown eyes.
I love nature because it's beautiful,
When I hear birds singing.
I want to remember the memories that make me happy.
Sometimes, I take care of nature in my garden.
I help my mum.
I am quiet
I'm kind and I like cats.
This is Rida!

Rida Anwar (7)
Oakdale Primary School, Stanground

My Dream Job

Different as a dodo.
Wise as a walrus.
Curious as a caterpillar.
Kind as a kangaroo.
Sly as a snow leopard.
Fantastic as a fox.
Trusting as a tortoise.
Brave as a bear.

All these things create my dream job.
A forensic scientist.
Now that's the top me.

Amelia Ihsan (10)
Oakdale Primary School, Stanground

Mysterious Animal

I can sometimes be vicious.
I live in underground dens.
I can make up to forty sounds.
I'm more like a cat than a dog.
I have impeccable hearing.
I'm extremely playful.
A group of me is called a skulk.
What am I?

Answer: A fox.

Laila Courten (10)
Oakdale Primary School, Stanground

Me!

I am...
Magically musical,
A great goalie,
Dependant on my lunatic friends,
Mischief maker,
Terrible baker,
Gamer,
Penalty saver,
Game creator,
Cat owner,
Cat fosterer,
Cat lover,
Animal lover,
Roblox gamer,
Cat tamer.

Ben Condon (10)
Oakdale Primary School, Stanground

Everything About Me

A kennings poem

I am a...
Quite good gamer.
Mischief maker.
Terrible baker.
Animal lover.
Game creator.
Cat owner.
Pokémon card collector.
Robux earner.
Quick learner.
Console owner.
Dazzling defender.
Space Jam lover.
This is me!

Luca Ignat (10)
Oakdale Primary School, Stanground

Henry, The Boss!

I am a brother,
Henry is my brother,
Henry is a super roller,
Henry is a crocodile biter,
Henry is as grabby as a crane,
Henry rules the house,
This is Henry,
But he is funny,
And cute,
I love him,
He is my brother.

Charlie Ellis (8)
Oakdale Primary School, Stanground

The Time

I am a star striker.
I am a sweet eater.
I hate bees,
And my cat is stinky,
And I just got a brand new phone,
Six months ago.
I am a nice guy,
But the most uncomfortable thing is my sister,
She's annoying.

Muhammad Kheir Alsafadi (8)
Oakdale Primary School, Stanground

This Is Me

I am a lover of chicken nuggets.
I am a lover of sweeties.
I am a lover of games.
I am a lover of maths.
I am a lover of Roblox.
I am a lover of a cup of tea.
I am a lover of school.
I am a lover of pizza.

Aistis Baratinskas (7)
Oakdale Primary School, Stanground

This Is Me

I am a superstar and a lightning bolt in football.
I love dogs very much.
A book lover
And as kind, as you could be.
A lifelong football fan.
Maths is my superpower.
I can always rely on my lunatic friends.

Jeevan Singh (10)
Oakdale Primary School, Stanground

Me, Molly

I am a...
Zebra liker,
Older sister,
Orange carrot eater.
Loyal, aspiring school leader.
Silly surreal drawer.
Fish eater.
Book reader.
Wanna be a songwriter.
This is me!

Molly Mcgroarty (10)
Oakdale Primary School, Stanground

Anger!

A nnoying little ball of stroppiness.
N ever means what she says.
G ives up and hates trying.
E motional disaster.
R eally you can't blame me for being myself!

Lacey Valentine (10)
Oakdale Primary School, Stanground

This Is Me

I love cars,
Just as I love football.
Cars are fast,
And it is a Land Rover Discovery Sport,
It goes super fast which makes me excited,
Just like my superhero,
Messi.

Freddie Worraker (7)
Oakdale Primary School, Stanground

This Is Me

My grandad is a hero to me.
My favourite animal is a tiger,
Because they are brave and heroic.
Just like Grandad.
I am kind, thoughtful and friendly,
Just like Grandad.

Nathan Carnegie (7)
Oakdale Primary School, Stanground

This Is A Part Of Me!

I am a basketball watcher.
I also like taking walks in Cardea.
I loved every minute of my birthday.
Miss Pfeiffer and Miss Kour are the best teachers ever.
This is me.

Alice Colbert (7)
Oakdale Primary School, Stanground

SBP

This is me.
I hate to sleep.
I love my brother.
Sometimes I play Fortnite.
My dad likes playing with me.
Exploring and I like apples.

Sam Pereira (7)
Oakdale Primary School, Stanground

This Is Me

S pecial to family and friends.
Y ellow is the colour of happiness, that's why I love it.
M ake friends every day.
P ositive thoughts are always needed.
A rt is one of my hobbies.
T olerant of everyone.
H onourable and helpful.
E nthusiastic about being there for others.
T rustworthy to others.
I make people laugh and smile.
C heering people up makes me happy.

Phoebe Elliott-Cannon (11)
Sandilands Primary School, Wythenshawe

All About Me

Haiku poetry

My name is Ruby,
I'm not as scared as Scooby,
I absorb sushi.

Cherish happiness,
From all the good times I've had,
And remember them.

I have a sweet tooth,
And a savoury one too,
I love chocolate.

Ruby Curness (10)
Sandilands Primary School, Wythenshawe

This Is Me

I nspire everyone.
N ever give up.
S upport your friends.
P ositive attitude.
I ntroduce your personality.
R each for the stars.
E ncourage others!

Ruby (10)
Sandilands Primary School, Wythenshawe

The Marvel Breakout

All of the gang came to Thor,
They realised they couldn't handle it anymore,
Galactus had got his way,
They had no way to play,
Thor said,
"I know it's hard, but we can't lose."
Storm had got a big bruise,
Mystique looked way too tired,
They all felt like they were going to get fired,
But then they started to think,
Oh yes, we can do this,
We shall not give up,
Let's go and get that win,
Galactus was here to win,
"Ah, they're getting in my way,
You have no time to play,
Now go!"
Iron Man repulsed,
Storm's loud wind.
"Yes, we did it!"

Evie-Rose Stayte (9)
St Joseph's Catholic Primary School, Carterton

Dinosaurs Winning A Tournament

Today was a tournament to the end,
The dinosaurs were depending on the game,
The first quarter game was against the Jerrys.
They had a lot of cherries.
They wanted to win,
They had teeth like a pin,
It was a game,
The Jerrys were so lame,
They won in extra time,
Then they had a lime,
The second game was against the Cherries,
Like they did against the Jerrys,
They won one to nil.
Their last game was against the Mangoes,
They last won against the Mangoes one to nil,
They started the game,
The Mangoes were so lame,
They started well,
Their best player was called Kell,

They scored,
They poured,
It was half time,
Someone said,
"It is mine."
It started again,
Someone farted,
The game was done,
"Love, it was one to nil to the Oranges."

Jaxon Archer (9)

St Joseph's Catholic Primary School, Carterton

My Imagination

A mermaid swam up in the sky,
Spotting a human trying to fly.
In a matter of seconds, she fell in love,
Flying to him like a dove.
"Hello there, sir, my name is Rose,
I can contract and also pose."
"Well hello there, you chubby old thing,
I'll cut your tail off and only one wing,
Please don't worry, it really won't hurt,
And by the way, my name is Bert."
"I'm sorry Bert, but not today.
Too bad now, right? I flew away!"
"Oh dang it now, I thought I had it,
Just wait till she needs my awesome sandpit!"

Chiara Connelly (10)
St Joseph's Catholic Primary School, Carterton

Where Did Wembley Go?

What? Where did Wembley go?
Looking, searching, meanwhile eating my dough.
News says 'where did Wembley go?'
"Well, I wasted my money."
"It's okay honey."
NASA is going to Mars,
Flying past the stars,
They land and what?
Wembley is on the planet Mars.
The news is back, with,
"Wembley is on Mars."
I'm watching this in my car with other cars,
NASA takes people to Mars,
And I'm still in the car beneath the stars.
"Can we go to Mars in a rocket?"
But I have no money in my pocket.

Sam Atkin (9)
St Joseph's Catholic Primary School, Carterton

The Star I Will Reach

The star that I will reach,
Will be on a beach,
Not swimming in the sea,
Or climbing up a tree,
But spending time with my whole entire family,
I hope to have some kids and pets,
If my pets are ill, I'll take them to the vets,
The star that I will reach,
I hope that God hears me preach,
I'll teach my kids how to be,
Kind to others, I hopefully see,
That God created us all equally,
The star that I will reach,
Is in a classroom, ready to teach,
I hope to teach kids like me,
To teach them to fly high in life, just like a bee.

Isobel Davies (10)
St Joseph's Catholic Primary School, Carterton

The Helicopter Bob

I once got a helicopter called Bob,
And I like flying up,
Up and up,
Look how high we are.
I once got a helicopter called Bob,
We flew high and high,
Through the clouds.
He used to say,
"One day, we will go to the moon."
On the other day,
We tried to go to the moon,
But we crashed into a poetry competition,
And Bob the helicopter said,
"My dear friend, this is goodbye."
And I won the poetry competition,
And with the money,
I repaired my helicopter,
And went to the moon.

Diego Gancalves (10)
St Joseph's Catholic Primary School, Carterton

Sammy The Footballer

Sammy the footballer,
Everything got smaller,
He was one of the best,
But never got any rest.
He was as fast as a lion,
His opponents would keep sighing but,
Sammy never looked back.

Tommy, his friend, was much of a class clown,
And he very much liked the sound of his own voice.
He was very impatient,
And Sammy didn't know why.
He was very sad.

Sammy once got very, very sad,
So he ran away,
And then Sammy,
Oh, Sammy,
Was never seen again.

Oscar Plywacz (10)
St Joseph's Catholic Primary School, Carterton

The Dog And The Rabbit

There once was a dog,
Who walked over a log,
He went for a walk one sunny day,
The leaves started blowing away,
Even though it was kind of chilly.
The dog saw a bunny,
And thought she looked kind of funny.
The bunny was scared,
The dog looked and stared.
They said they were good friends.
They saw a pie on the windowsill.
The lady said there is one hundred mill.
They sat down and ate the pie,
Even though the night was nigh.
They stayed with each other forever.

Ella Kearsey (10)

St Joseph's Catholic Primary School, Carterton

Halloween Is The Best

H alloween is my favourite holiday, this is because
it is a spooky day.
A ll of this crammed in a short amount of time.
L iars say, "This day makes my brain go away."
L uminous green lit up the dark,
O minous glows scare the kids.
W inners are the people who get a lot of sweets.
E veryone's excited for Halloween, even though
you get cavities.
E ven the adults are excited.
N ot even the spoilt kids.

Riley Beal (10)
St Joseph's Catholic Primary School, Carterton

About Me

This is about the things I like,
I usually like riding a bike,
My favourite animal is a penguin,
I like it when they waddle,
I quite like jumping in a puddle,
I really like drawing mushrooms,
Mostly the red ones,
I support Liverpool,
And I like going swimming in a pool,
I really like the colour yellow,
That's why mostly everything is yellow,
I love flowers,
I like having showers,
I love bright colours,
So I like the sun.

Isabelle Finnemore (10)
St Joseph's Catholic Primary School, Carterton

The Bee And The Worm

There once was a worm,
That didn't like fun.
Until she saw a bee,
That was stuck in a tree,
She didn't show luck, but,
Instead, she looked at a truck,
What a fabulous bee looking at me.

She slithered up the tree,
To try and save the bee,
Instead, the bee flew,
To a slimy mountain, the bee's head,
Stuck, to go and find a duck,
To try to get the bee.
So that's why the bee went into the tree.

Maria Grzywacz (10)
St Joseph's Catholic Primary School, Carterton

The World Is An End

The world was ended,
The world was an end.
It was too much to handle,
This was going too far,
Hopefully, it would end,
Then a small living thing went,
Up to the fire,
It looked like a rat or a cat,
It didn't scream or scurry,
Then a fluffy fat cat,
Who came in a hat,
Who had a bat,
It gave a bit of tat,
The fire was flicking up,
Oh no, this was a big no,
As for the world,
It ended.

Joana Pedro (9)
St Joseph's Catholic Primary School, Carterton

The Lion At The Zoo

I'm walking through the zoo,
There's so much to do,
Even though I'm a lion,
I walk past babies crying,
The first house to see,
It's a horrible place to be,
There's a beautiful and wonderful feast,
People are looking at me like I am a beast,
They say hello and run away,
But they stop and have a lay,
I say stop and then put them in my pie,
Others pass me by again so I say hi,
Then bye.

Janey Jupp (10)
St Joseph's Catholic Primary School, Carterton

Little Miss Perfect!

Once there was a girl,
Who liked to twirl.
The sky was blue.
The sky was grey,
Maybe it will be pretty someday.
Maybe on Sunday.
Maybe on Monday.
Sundays are happy and great,
But then on Monday came an earthquake.
That was why Mondays are so terrible,
And that is why Monday was so memorable.
She danced away as she played,
And then went to bed the next day...
The end of Little Miss Perfect!

Mia Garthwaite (9)
St Joseph's Catholic Primary School, Carterton

The Earth

The world will end,
We've gone too far,
Because of pollution,
Nothing was done.
It was all good before we started,
Doing pollution and deforestation.
Finally, something was done,
Stopped using plastic.
Oh my,
We still have a chance,
Help us save our life,
The Earth was our home,
For millions of years,
Don't ruin our chance,
The Earth was saved at last.

Amdia Paul (9)
St Joseph's Catholic Primary School, Carterton

Life Is Hard

Life is hard.
For some people, it is like a blank card.
They have never seen anything but the dark.
Some memories leave a mark.
Nothing can fix it.
No happiness, not a bit.
It may be tough,
But nothing is enough.
Until it all comes to an end.
You find that one friend.
They stop your fear,
And are always near,
And say nothing can hurt you.
I feel it too.

Lacey Marshall (10)
St Joseph's Catholic Primary School, Carterton

My Life

There was a boy called Tom who liked Mars,
And flew there in a car,
Which had a bunch of bars,
His father had a bunch of scars.
His father liked to do bids,
He had loads of kids.
Tom liked to build rockets,
That had a bunch of sockets.
They travelled to the moon on the pig,
They got there in zero minutes.

Charlie Farthing (9)
St Joseph's Catholic Primary School, Carterton

The Seaside And The Whale

The whale went to sea,
He saw a tasty bee,
That was his afternoon snack,
Then he went back,
The whale was blue,
Then he caught the flu,
He woke up,
The whale got ready,
And he was steady,
The sea was warm,
The bubbles didn't form,
He headed off,
He started to cough.

Sophia Oliver (11)
St Joseph's Catholic Primary School, Carterton

Artsy, That's Me

A rtsy is me, full of creativity, it comes so naturally!
D ogs and cats are adorable.
V ery silly, I'm full of joy and fun.
E lephants are my mum's favourite animal.
N ature is something I love, animals are the best.
T ea, my family loves it.
U nderneath my blanket is my favourite place to be.
R eading is fun, like a whole other world, mysteries are my favourite though.
O bviously, I'm not good at everything.
U sually, I just do art.
S chool is not the best, although I like going.

Ophelia Green (10)
St Nicholas Elstree Primary School, Elstree

The Arsenal Rap

Saka, Bergkamp, Wrighty, Cole
The lists of legends go on and on
But for me it's easy, Thierry Henry
Remember the Arsenal back in 03
This is me
Ohh
This is me
My team play in red and white
It's not United
It's my Arsenal
Every team that steps foot on our field
Our cannon shoots them home
Arsenal are massive, everywhere they go.
That's my Arsenal
Ohh
That's my Arsenal.
We fly our flag, high and above
Between me and them it's more than love.

Ollie Brown (11)
St Nicholas Elstree Primary School, Elstree

This Is Me

Hi, I'm very sporty
And I'm four times younger than forty.
You can't consider me very dorky
And I'm the opposite of someone porky.
I go to school because I'm cool.
I do sports, swimming most of all
Which is hosted inside the venue pool.
I like literacy and I'm not a fool.
I went to the beach and found a shell that's alive.
It can move one centimetre before I count to fifty-five.
Guess what it is,
I want your best try.
It's my favourite animal,
Just don't ask me why.

Elijah Wright (10)
St Nicholas Elstree Primary School, Elstree

Summer Holidays

Summer holidays are the best!
A time we have a break from school,
And have a rest.
Packing my bags full to the brim,
Getting my hair done, trim, trim, trim.
Going on a plane,
Drifting through the sky.
How amazing,
The planes can fly.
Going to the beach,
Seeing all the colourful fish.
Mmm, it's delish.
Ice lollies melting in a hurry,
Looking at it drip.
In the sky,
Red, orange and yellow,
Makes me feel all nice and mellow.

Adela Pocelajlova (10)
St Nicholas Elstree Primary School, Elstree

Pizza Is Life

P ink dragon fruit is the best.
I ce cream is best in heaps.
Z elda: Breath of the Wild is a good game.
Z oos are cool.
A nimals are my favourite.

I cing is best on cakes.
S pelling is my weak spot.

L iving calculator.
I mpatient I am.
F ractions are easy.
E asy maths is unheard of.

Mark Bazgan (9)
St Nicholas Elstree Primary School, Elstree

This Is Me

Summer is the best,
Because we have lots of time to rest.
I go to school,
Because I am cool.
I like cats,
And I wear odd hats.
When I am down,
I get back off the ground.
Animals are free,
Because of me.
Ice lollies are yummy,
And they steam up my tummy.
The clouds up in the sky,
Are like a cotton candy delight.

Ellenor Peters (10)
St Nicholas Elstree Primary School, Elstree

This Is Me!

I am fiddly but silly.
I love animals,
Rabbits the best.
They jump really high,
Put it to the test.
I am fast and funny.
I am curious and chaotic,
That's what they say.
But my friends say I'm nice, hooray.
I am excited and eager.
I am adventurous and annoying.
I am untidy but lively.
This is me.

Tianna Trainor (8)
St Nicholas Elstree Primary School, Elstree

Halloween

H alloween is the time to trick or treat.
A pple bobbing, caramel apples.
L icking candy.
L ooking for treats.
O dd costumes.
W orld filled with laughter.
E vents happening everywhere.
E arning lots of sweets.
N ow we can go home.

Kyra Alexis-Crearer (10)
St Nicholas Elstree Primary School, Elstree

This Is Me

T ell some jokes.
H ave faith in my friends.
I like playing with my friends.
S ometimes can be annoying.

I nearly never give up.
S illy to my friends.

M y favourite colour is lime.
E ngland is where I live.

Alexander Cierniak (10)
St Nicholas Elstree Primary School, Elstree

The Boys In Blue

The boys in blue,
I'm a fan, it's true.
Mason Mount on the ball.
When he gets it, he will score.
Stamford Bridge.
It's where they play.
They're bringing it all the way,
When people are there to shoot the ball,
Mendy is there just like a brick wall.

Ernest Peca (10)
St Nicholas Elstree Primary School, Elstree

My Favourite Things

My favourite things, the gleaming sunset.
My number one, dogs and cats.
I am nice to all the people I've met
And I give my cats ten thousand pats.

I love to sing music.
I have made good friends.
I hate being sick
And I know how to make amends.

Bethany Brittain (10)
St Nicholas Elstree Primary School, Elstree

Summer Is Here

Summer is the best.
Waiting for ice lollies to arrive in a nest,
Pool cold like the North Pole.
Floats floating on a cool pool.
Remember to put sunscreen on,
And you won't get hurt by the sun's beams.
People get ready to go in the sun to have fun.

Romy Hutchin (10)
St Nicholas Elstree Primary School, Elstree

Football Is The Best

F ootball is cool.
O n the pitch, we play football and it's great.
O scar R is the best.
T iarah is my friend.
B alls are cool.
A ll people are the best.
L illy is my friend.
L ogan is my friend.

Oscar Sartori (7)
St Nicholas Elstree Primary School, Elstree

This Is Me

F un and awesome.
R espectful.
I ndependent sometimes.
E nglish is my favourite.
N ever give up.
D reams are to work at an animal shelter.
L oving and caring.
Y ellow is one of my favourite colours.

Naya-Tate Mclaughlin (10)
St Nicholas Elstree Primary School, Elstree

This Is Me

I like to rest.
Giraffes are the best.
Giraffes rule.
They are so cool.
They don't have the look of a mule.
Have they ever splashed in a pool?
I also like my tablet
And that is when I'm adequate.
I'm trustful
Also helpful.

Ivy Bennett (8)
St Nicholas Elstree Primary School, Elstree

Home

Home is the best place,
Where I do everything at my own pace.
The place where I eat, sleep and drink,
I don't feel at the edge of an ice rink.
There, I can relax for hours and hours,
I can unwind, dream and pretend to have superpowers.

Jood Sayarh (10)
St Nicholas Elstree Primary School, Elstree

This Is Me

F izzy Fanta is forever fabulous.
A mazing Fanta makes you jump!
"N o more," said your mum.
T ickling your tastebuds.
A sk your friends if they want some...

Antonia Gavriliuc (7)
St Nicholas Elstree Primary School, Elstree

This Is Me

H aving fun is the best.
A good friend is what you need.
P roud is a good feeling.
P enguins are extremely fluffy.
Y es, this is me.

Alex Joslin (8)
St Nicholas Elstree Primary School, Elstree

This Is Me

A little girl who can have many dreams but only has one dream.
A sister who loves and annoys my sibling.
A sporty person with many hopes of winning a competition.
A person who loves everyone in any way, shape, form or colour.
The eldest sibling that has loads of responsibilities.
I am an overprotective kid who had one fear: losing friends.
A little girl who has a mum that believes in me.
A nice kid who believes in myself and wants everyone to be who they want to be.
A ten-year-old artist who loves to have my things published.
A person who cares for their things.
A sounding cymbal who never gives up on my only dream.
A person who feels to be a singer or artist or hopefully both.

A ten-year-old who is going to year seven soon and has to go away from friends.
This is me.

Lacey Preston (10)
Valence Primary School, Dagenham

This Is Me

M y name is Michael and I write like a Kardashian, this is me.
I have three brothers and they are trouble sometimes, this is me.
C an I train pets? Yes, indeed I can, this is me.
H elp some people like it's a disability, this is me.
A helping hand if needed, this is me.
E veryone I treat like family, this is me.
L ike every animal, even pets, this is me.

I do like to write but not a lot,
Because my hand will start to hurt a lot.
And I wear glasses and I can't see,
Or think properly if everybody,
Is talking and screaming.
But now, I can concentrate.

Michael Gregory (10)
Valence Primary School, Dagenham

This Is Me

A rt fanatical lover.
N ot a lover of annoying people.
A mazing at walkovers and drawing.
S ignificant and lovely friend of all.
T alks a lot about everything.
A n emotional dance lover.
S uch a gymnastics dance fan but,
I rresponsible to other people.
J oyful and happy all the time.
A lover of good friends.

Silly sometimes, but not for long.
Motivational and pretty person.
Irresponsible to some annoying people.
No criticism accepted.
Daydreamer all the time,
This is me.

Anastasija Gurska (10)
Valence Primary School, Dagenham

Jujitsu Jasmine

J ujitsu and karate are what I protect myself with.
A dancer on Wednesday and Friday, breaking the laws of dance.
S wimming like a shark with a broken arm.
M usic is my world, but sad music is my enemy.
I ndian girl by father.
N ightly scientist, writer by day.
E nchanted by writing and Roald Dahl.

Runs through my veins,
Writing is pure passion.
Bluebelt in karate.
This is me, a revolutionary reader.

Jasmine Lakhanpal (10)
Valence Primary School, Dagenham

This Is Me

Excited to be here,
But has a frown on his face.
Why is he unhappy?
His secret is not safe.
No one said he's perfect,
But who are you to judge?
Someone has blessed him,
Someone from above.
His mind is exploding,
With some sort of thing,
Because he likes to sing,
Well, there's me,
And as you can see,
This is me, this is me, this is me.

Ethan Allison (10)
Valence Primary School, Dagenham

This Is Me

I am an exquisite football player with outstanding power.
I am as tall as a tower and as fierce as a tiger.
I am so strong I can stall a boulder,
Even as I get older.
I am always thinking,
And it doesn't give me time to start blinking.
I am so smart, I can write any kind of maths,
And always find the answer to them.
This is me.

Jason Murataj (10)
Valence Primary School, Dagenham

I Am A Forest

I am a forest.
Wild, untamed, free
And naturally deceiving.
An endless network of twists and turns,
Never knowing where you might end up.
For I am a forest, no liar or thief.

I'm just a forest, naturally deceiving.

Amari Williams (9)
Valence Primary School, Dagenham

Who I Am

A football player in disguise.
S cotland forever.
I play as striker.
M o Salah, my guy.

Asim Mutiur-Rahman (9)
Valence Primary School, Dagenham

YOUNG WRITERS INFORMATION

We hope you have enjoyed reading this book – and that you will continue to in the coming years.

If you're the parent or family member of an enthusiastic poet or story writer, do visit our website **www.youngwriters.co.uk/subscribe** and sign up to receive news, competitions, writing challenges and tips, activities and much, much more! There's lots to keep budding writers motivated!

If you would like to order further copies of this book, or any of our other titles, then please give us a call or order via your online account.

Young Writers
Remus House
Coltsfoot Drive
Peterborough
PE2 9BF
(01733) 890066
info@youngwriters.co.uk

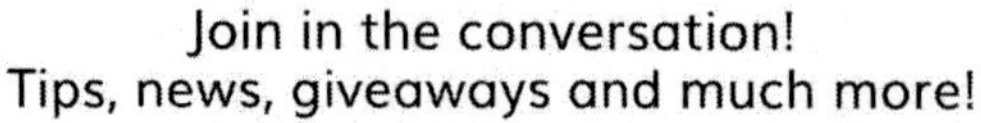

Join in the conversation!
Tips, news, giveaways and much more!